# picnics

# picnics

simple recipes for eating outdoors

RYLAND
PETERS
& SMALL

LONDON NEW YORK

First published in the United States
in 2005
by Ryland Peters & Small, Inc.
519 Broadway, 5th Floor
New York, NY 10012
www.rylandpeters.com

10 9 8 7 6 5 4 3 2 1

Printed in China

**Senior Designer** Steve Painter
**Commissioning Editor**
Elsa Petersen-Schepelern
**Editor** Sharon Cochrane
**Production** Sheila Smith
**Picture Research** Tracy Ogino
**Art Director** Gabriella Le Grazie
**Publishing Director** Alison Starling

Library of Congress Cataloging-in-
Publication Data

Picnics / Linda Collister ... [et al.].
    p. cm.
  Includes index.
  ISBN 1-84172-816-0
  1.  Barbecue cookery. 2.  Picnicking.  I.
Collister, Linda.
  TX840.B3P5255 2005
  641.5'78--dc22

                                    2004020522

**Notes**
• All spoon measurements are level
unless otherwise specified.
• Uncooked or partly cooked eggs
should not be served to the very young,
the very old, those with compromised
immune systems, or to pregnant women.
• Before baking, weigh or measure all
ingredients exactly and prepare baking
pans or trays.
• Ovens should be preheated to the
specified temperature.

# contents

# the perfect picnic

Choose a spot for your picnic that's easy to get to, preferably close to where you can park the car. It's all very well planning a romantic picnic at the top of a mountain, but don't forget that a picnic basket can get very heavy, very quickly!

## comfort

• If you are traveling by car, take light, collapsible tables and chairs.

• Take plenty of blankets and pillows.

• Choose a shady place to spread your picnic blanket.

• Pack lanterns, flashlights, and citronella candles if you will still be outdoors in the evening.

## storage

• Safety and convenience are the most important elements when it comes to packing the food.

• Use coolers. Line the bottom with freezer packs and put raw ingredients on top of them and more delicate items at the top. This is also the best method for carrying ice cubes.

• Refrigerate pre-cooked or prepared food until ready to pack.

• Remove marinated meat or fish from the refrigerator one hour before cooking to let it return to room temperature. It will cook more quickly, reducing the risk of undercooking and spoiling.

• Chill and store the food in the same container; plastic containers, zip-lock bags, and vacuum flasks are all good. Plastic or glass bottles are ideal for drinks, dressings, or syrups.

• Wrap sandwiches and rolls in wax paper, then in foil. Store and transport cakes in their pans.

• Hardware and office supply stores sell aluminum storage pans, which are ideal for small snack dishes. Most homes have empty chocolate tins and cookie tins somewhere in the pantry, which are great for transporting cookies and cakes.

• Remember to take along a bag in which to bring home any trash after the picnic.

## transport

• Picnic baskets are romantic, but often impractical. When full, they're very heavy and difficult for one person to carry. Two-handled baskets are preferable because you can share the load.

• Use paper plates and plastic cups—or glasses and plates wrapped individually in paper towels or cloth to avoid breakage.

• For adventurous picnic destinations, pack non-perishable foods that can be eaten with your fingers to save having to carry a heavy pack. A backpack is the easiest way to transport lunch if you are walking a long distance or going up or down steep hills.

# picnic from market stalls

**Menu suggestions**

prosciutto

salami

potato and tarragon cake

mixed washed salad greens

pâté en croûte

sliced ham and parsley mousse

pissaladière

bread

goat cheese

peaches

chocolate opera cake

apple custard tart

hazelnut cookies

vanilla yogurts

**To drink**

hard cider

old-fashioned lemonade

## market shopping

If you don't have the time to cook what you need for your picnic, or you just fancy spoiling yourself, visit your local outdoor market, if your town has one, or a nearby farmers' market. Sometimes the people who have made or grown the food are on the stalls selling their own goods, so you can chat about what is available. It's such a treat, as well as being a very sensual experience, to shop for food at market stalls. It often looks so raw and real, with the stallholders full of stories and love for their produce. Don't be afraid to ask questions—they invariably have a wealth of information that they are often only too happy to share.

The menu on the left is just to give you an idea of what you might find at market stalls to create an instant, no-cook picnic. Delicacies will vary from place to place, but it's always fun to be adventurous and try something that you're not familiar with, be it a cheese, pâté, tart, or simply an unusual bread.

## the scene

After gathering your purchases together in baskets, boxes, and bags, you will need to find a quiet, shady spot for you to set up your picnic. Spread out a large, pretty cloth, and put out all the delicious produce on it for everyone to unwrap. Sit back and enjoy your no-cook *al fresco* feast.

## the style

This is really made by the surroundings and the goods you buy. Some food producers take such pride in their packaging and presentation—beautiful sheets of paper to wrap meats and cheeses; pretty boxes to protect tarts and cakes; crisp, paper bags for bread; and pretty baskets for fruit. All you need is a beautiful picnic blanket or cloth on which to set out your feast, plus utensils, glasses, napkins, and the all-important corkscrew.

Chickpeas are a fantastic ingredient, but unfortunately most people don't really know what to do with them. Buying canned chickpeas, as in this super Mediterranean-style salad, dispenses with the need to soak them, making them so easy to use.

5 plum tomatoes, cut in half and seeded

3 large red bell peppers, cut in half and seeded

2 cups canned chickpeas, rinsed and drained

a bunch of flat-leaf parsley

sea salt and freshly ground black pepper

extra virgin olive oil, to serve

**Serves 4**

# chickpea, tomato, and bell pepper salad

Lightly oil a roasting pan and add the tomatoes and bell peppers to it. Cook in a preheated oven at 375°F for 20 minutes.

Remove from the oven and transfer the tomatoes and peppers to a bowl. Add the drained chickpeas, then mix in the parsley and season with salt and pepper. Let cool.

Transfer the salad to an airtight container. When you are ready to eat, sprinkle with a little olive oil, and serve.

# salads and vegetarian

# fava bean salad
# with mint and parmesan

Great for picnics, this salad can also be served as part of a tapas spread, as an appetizer, or snack. If it's early in the season and you have young, tender fava beans, it's not necessary to peel them after blanching. If you can't find fresh fava beans, use green beans instead and cut them into 1-inch lengths.

1½ lb. shelled, young fresh
fava beans, about 5 cups

3 heads Belgian endives

leaves from 3 sprigs of mint

½ cup Parmesan cheese shavings

**Hazelnut oil dressing**

2 tablespoons extra virgin olive oil

¼ cup hazelnut oil*

2 teaspoons white wine vinegar

1 teaspoon Dijon mustard

¼ teaspoon sugar

sea salt and freshly ground
black pepper

**Serves 6**

Plunge the fava beans into a saucepan of lightly salted, boiling water, return to a boil, and simmer for 1 to 2 minutes. Drain and refresh the beans immediately under cold running water. Pat dry and peel away the gray-green outer skin, if necessary. Put the peeled beans in a large airtight container.

Cut the endives in half lengthwise, slice thickly crosswise, then add to the beans. Add the mint leaves, tearing any large ones in half, then sprinkle the shavings of Parmesan over the salad.

Put all the dressing ingredients in a screw-top jar and shake well to mix.

Just before serving, shake the dressing well and sprinkle it over the salad. Toss well and serve.

*Note If hazelnut oil is difficult to find, substitute extra virgin olive oil. Buy nut oils in small quantities and store them in the refrigerator: they are delicate, and become rancid very quickly.

This refreshing summer salad with a bright note of fresh mint makes a superb accompaniment to cold meat or fish.

# zucchini, feta, and mint salad

1 tablespoon sesame seeds

6 medium zucchini

3 tablespoons extra virgin olive oil

6 oz. feta cheese, crumbled, about 1½ cups

a handful of fresh mint leaves

sea salt and freshly ground black pepper

**Dressing**

¼ cup extra virgin olive oil

1 tablespoon freshly squeezed lemon juice

1 small garlic clove, crushed

**Serves 4**

Put the sesame seeds in a dry skillet and toast over medium heat until golden and aromatic. Remove from the pan, let cool, and store in an airtight container.

Cut the zucchini diagonally into thick slices. Put the slices in a bowl, sprinkle with the olive oil, season with salt and pepper, and toss well. Cook on a hot stove-top grill pan for 2 to 3 minutes on each side until charred and tender. Remove from the pan and let cool.

Put all the dressing ingredients in a screw-top jar. Add salt and pepper to taste and shake well.

Put the zucchini, feta, and mint in a large airtight container. When ready to serve, shake the dressing and pour it over the salad. Toss well. Sprinkle with the toasted sesame seeds and serve at once.

Ready-made tapenade is available in supermarkets and gourmet stores and is usually quite good quality. Some stores make their own and these are definitely worth seeking out, but make it yourself if you have the time.

# pasta, squash, and feta salad with olive dressing

¼ cup pumpkin seeds

1½ lb. butternut squash

1 tablespoon extra virgin olive oil

1 tablespoon chopped fresh thyme leaves

I lb. dried penne pasta

10 oz. feta cheese, diced, about 2½ cups

10 oz. cherry tomatoes, about 2 cups, cut in half

¼ cup chopped fresh basil

sea salt and freshly ground black pepper

**Olive dressing**

½ cup extra virgin olive oil

3 tablespoons tapenade (page 35)

freshly squeezed juice of 1 lemon

1 teaspoon honey

**Serves 6**

Put the pumpkin seeds in a dry skillet and toast over medium heat until golden and aromatic. Remove from the heat, let cool, and store in an airtight container.

Peel and seed the butternut squash and cut the flesh into bite-size pieces. Put in a bowl or plastic bag and add the oil, thyme, salt, and pepper. Toss well, then arrange in a single layer in a roasting pan. Roast in a preheated oven at 400°F for 25 minutes, or until golden and tender. Remove from the oven and let cool.

To make the dressing, put the olive oil, tapenade, lemon juice, and honey in a bowl. Beat well, then add salt and pepper to taste.

Bring a large saucepan of lightly salted water to a boil, add the penne, and cook for 8 to 9 minutes, or according to the timings on the package, until *al dente* (just cooked but still slightly crunchy in the middle). Drain well, then immediately stir in ¼ cup of the dressing. Let cool. Put the remaining dressing in a screw-top jar.

When cool, put the pasta and squash in an airtight container, mix gently, then add the feta cheese, cherry tomatoes, and basil. Just before serving, stir in the toasted pumpkin seeds and the remaining dressing.

With its lovely, earthy flavors, a frittata is an Italian version of the Spanish tortilla or the French omelette. Different ingredients are added depending upon the region or season.

# mixed mushroom frittata

3 tablespoons extra virgin olive oil

2 shallots, finely chopped (if unavailable, use 2 tablespoons minced mild onions)

2 garlic cloves, finely chopped

1 tablespoon chopped fresh thyme leaves

3 cups mixed wild and cultivated mushrooms, such as chanterelle, portobello, shiitake, and white button mushrooms

6 eggs

2 tablespoons chopped, fresh flat-leaf parsley

sea salt and freshly ground black pepper

**Serves 6**

Put 2 tablespoons of the oil in a nonstick skillet, heat gently, then add the shallots, garlic, and thyme. Gently sauté for 5 minutes until softened but not browned.

Meanwhile, brush off any dirt clinging to the mushrooms and wipe the caps. Chop or slice coarsely and add to the skillet. Sauté for 4 to 5 minutes until just starting to release their juices. Remove the skillet from the heat.

Put the eggs in a bowl along with the parsley and a little salt and pepper, beat briefly, then stir in the mushroom mixture. Wipe the skillet clean with paper towels.

Heat the remaining tablespoon of oil in the clean skillet and pour in the egg and mushroom mixture. Cook over medium heat for 8 to 10 minutes until set on the bottom. Transfer the skillet to a preheated broiler and cook the frittata for 2 to 3 minutes until the top is set and spotted brown. Let cool, then wrap in wax paper.

Blue cheese and walnuts are a great combination. The blue cheese imparts a wonderful richness of flavor to this light, creamy tart with walnut crust.

# roquefort and walnut tart

¼ cup walnuts

½ cup all-purpose flour, plus extra for dusting

1 teaspoon salt

¼ cup butter, chilled and diced

**Filling**

½ cup Roquefort cheese, chopped

1 cup ricotta cheese

½ cup heavy cream

3 eggs, lightly beaten

2 tablespoons walnut oil

sea salt and freshly ground black pepper

*a tart pan, 9 inches diameter, buttered*
*parchment paper*
*baking beans or uncooked rice*

**Serves 6**

To make the pastry dough crust, put the walnuts in a dry skillet and cook for 1 to 2 minutes over medium heat until they start to smell toasted. Transfer to a bowl and let cool. When cool, transfer to a food processor or blender and grind to a meal. Sift the flour and salt into a bowl and rub in the butter with the tips of your fingers until the mixture resembles fine bread crumbs. Stir in the ground walnuts and then enough cold water to form a soft dough, 1 to 2 tablespoons. Transfer the dough to a lightly floured counter, knead gently, then shape into a flat circle. Wrap in plastic wrap and chill in the refrigerator for about 30 minutes.

Put the dough on a lightly floured counter, roll out to a circle about 12 inches in diameter, and line the tart pan with it. Prick the bottom of the crust all over with a fork and chill for another 30 minutes.

Line the dough crust with parchment paper and add some baking beans or rice. Bake in a preheated oven at 400°F for 10 minutes. Remove the paper, and beans or rice, and bake for another 5 to 6 minutes until the crust is crisp and lightly golden. Remove from the oven and let cool for about 10 minutes. Leave the oven on.

Meanwhile, to prepare the filling, put the Roquefort in a food processor along with the ricotta, cream, eggs, walnut oil, salt, and pepper. Blend briefly until mixed but not smooth. Pour into the tart crust and cook in the preheated oven for about 20 minutes until risen and golden. Remove from the oven and let cool in the pan.

What is it about caramelized onions? They smell just divine, especially when cooked in butter. These simple onion tarts, topped with creamy goat cheese, can be eaten warm, although they are also good served cold for picnics.

# onion, thyme, and goat cheese tarts

3 tablespoons butter

1 lb. onions, thinly sliced, about 4 cups

2 garlic cloves, crushed

1 tablespoon chopped fresh thyme leaves

¾ lb. puff pastry dough, defrosted if frozen

all-purpose flour, for dusting

8 oz. log of goat cheese

sea salt and freshly ground black pepper

*a baking tray*

**Makes 8**

Put the butter in a skillet and melt over low heat. Add the onions, garlic, and thyme, and sauté gently for 20 to 25 minutes until softened and golden. Season to taste with salt and pepper. Remove the skillet from the heat and let cool.

Put the dough on a lightly floured counter and roll out to form a rectangle, 8 x 6 inches, trimming the edges. Cut the rectangle in half lengthwise and into 4 crosswise, making 8 pieces in total, each one about 4 inches square.

Divide the onion mixture between the squares spreading it over the top, leaving a thin border around the edges. Cut the cheese into 8 slices and arrange 1 slice in the center of each square.

Transfer the squares to a large baking tray and bake in a preheated oven at 425°F for 12 to 15 minutes until the dough has risen and the goat cheese is golden. Remove from the oven and let cool.

# focaccia topped with cherry tomatoes and pesto

1 cake compressed yeast, 0.6 oz.
or 1 envelope rapid-rise yeast,
¼ oz.

a pinch of sugar

2⅔ cups all-purpose flour,
plus extra for dusting

1 teaspoon salt, plus extra
for cooking

2 tablespoons extra virgin olive oil,
plus extra for sprinkling

6 oz. cherry tomatoes, cut in half,
about 1½ cups

¼ cup pitted black olives, such as
niçoise, cut in half

**Pesto**

1 cup basil leaves

1 garlic clove, crushed

2 tablespoons pine nuts

⅓ cup extra virgin olive oil

2 tablespoons freshly grated
Parmesan cheese

sea salt and freshly ground
black pepper

*a baking pan, 8 x 12 inches*

**Serves 8**

**The secret to making focaccia is to let the dough rise three times rather than twice, as you would for regular bread dough. It is well worth the extra 30 minutes needed, as the result is light, airy, and totally delicious.**

If you are using fresh yeast, put it in a small bowl, add the sugar and ¾ cup warm water, and stir until the yeast has dissolved. Add 2 tablespoons of the flour and put in a warm place for 10 minutes until frothy. Sift the remaining flour and the salt into a bowl. Add the frothed yeast mixture and oil and mix until a dough forms.

If using dry yeast, put the yeast, sugar, flour, salt, and oil in a large bowl and add ¾ cup warm water. Mix until a dough forms.

Transfer the dough to a lightly floured counter and knead for 10 minutes until smooth and elastic. Shape the dough into a ball, transfer to an oiled bowl, cover with plastic wrap, and let the dough rise for 1 hour or until doubled in size.

Transfer the dough to a lightly floured counter, knead gently, then shape or roll into a rectangle to fit snugly into the baking pan. Cover and let rise for 30 minutes. Using your fingers, press indentations all over the surface of the dough. Cover again and let rise for another hour until well risen.

Meanwhile, to make the pesto, put the basil leaves, garlic, pine nuts, and oil in a food processor and purée to form a vivid green paste. Transfer to a bowl and stir in the cheese and salt and pepper to taste.

Spread 2 to 3 tablespoons of the pesto carefully over the risen dough without letting it collapse. Put the tomatoes and olives on top and sprinkle with a little more oil and about ½ tablespoon salt. Bake in a preheated oven at 400°F for about 25 minutes until risen and golden. Remove from the pan and let cool on a wire rack.

breads and dips

Fougasse belongs to the same ancient family of breads as *focaccie*, the original hearth breads. In Provence, these flat, slashed "ladder breads" (so called because of their shape) are highly decorative and often flavored with olives or herbs. Their unusual shape makes them easy to pull apart—ideal for picnics.

# fougasse

¼ cup extra virgin olive oil, plus extra for baking

2 cups warm water

2 teaspoons honey (optional)

1¾ cups whole-wheat flour (or 1½ cups whole-wheat flour plus ⅓ cup buckwheat, triticale, or spelt flour)

1 teaspoon diastate malt

3¾ cups bread flour, plus extra for kneading

1 envelope rapid-rise yeast, ¼ oz.

2 teaspoons salt

**Toppings, your choice of:**

sliced garlic

onion rings

black olives, cut into strips

unwaxed orange zest, thinly sliced

orange-flower water

*2 large baking trays, oiled*

**Makes 4 loaves**

Put the oil, water, and honey, if using, in a measuring cup and stir to dissolve. Put the flour or flours, yeast, and salt in a food processor. With the motor running, pour the liquid through the feed tube to form a dense dough. Stop, then repeat for 30 seconds more, to develop the gluten.

Transfer the dough to a large, oiled bowl, and cover with an oiled plastic bag. Leave in a warm place for at least 30 minutes or up to 2 hours until the dough has doubled in volume.

Punch down the risen dough, transfer to a well-floured counter, and knead for 5 to 8 minutes or until silky and smooth. Return to the bowl, cover as before, and let rise again for 20 minutes or until doubled in size, then divide into 4. Squeeze, pat, and knead one ball into an oval. Transfer the oval to an oiled baking sheet, and pat or roll it out until it is 3 times its original size, and about ½ inch thick. Repeat the process with the second fougasse.

Make 2 rows of diagonal slashes in the dough, then open up the slashes to make larger holes. Tug out at the ends and sides if you would like to open up the dough even more.

Brush the two breads all over with olive oil, then sprinkle with warm water. Add your choice of garlic, onion, olives, orange zest, or orange-flower water.

Bake each fougasse towards the top of a preheated oven at 425°F for 15 to 20 minutes or until risen, crusty but still chewy. Repeat with the other 2 portions of dough.

Eat with your fingers, pulling the bread into short lengths.

4 ciabatta rolls

2 garlic cloves, crushed

¼ cup extra virgin olive oil

1 tablespoon red wine vinegar

4 ripe tomatoes, thickly sliced

1 can tuna in olive oil, 6¼ oz.,
drained and flaked

24 pitted black olives,
preferably niçoise

12 anchovy fillets in oil, drained

2 tablespoons capers

a few arugula leaves

a handful of basil leaves

sea salt and freshly ground
black pepper

**Serves 4**

Traditionally, pan bagnat, from Nice in the South of France, is made in a large baguette. This recipe uses Italian ciabatta rolls instead, which are slightly easier to transport. They are great for a picnic because they are wrapped in advance and all ready to go.

# pan bagnat

Cut the ciabatta rolls in half. Put the garlic, oil, and vinegar in a bowl, mix well, then brush all over the cut surfaces of the rolls.

Divide the remaining ingredients between the 4 rolls, add the lids, and wrap in plastic wrap. Let the rolls soak and infuse for at least 1 hour before serving.

This loaf packed with grilled vegetables, pesto, and goat cheese is a really tasty alternative to regular sandwiches. Make it a day ahead so it can be pressed overnight in the refrigerator for the flavors to develop and mingle.

# stuffed picnic loaf

1 round loaf of bread, about 9 inches diameter, 4 inches high

2 tablespoons extra virgin olive oil

½ quantity Pesto (page 24)

2 large red onions

2 large red bell peppers

2 large zucchini

8 oz. soft goat cheese, diced, 1½–2 cups

12 large basil leaves

sea salt and freshly ground black pepper

**Serves 6**

Cut the top off the loaf and carefully scoop out most of the bread, leaving just the outer shell (reserve the bread and use for another dish such as Taramasalata, page 34). Put 1 tablespoon of the oil in a bowl, stir in the pesto, and spread half the mixture around the inside of the shell and on the cut side of the lid. Set aside.

Cut the onions into wedges, brush with a little of the remaining oil, and cook on a preheated outdoor grill or on a stove-top grill pan for 10 minutes on each side until very tender. Let cool.

Cook the peppers on the preheated grill or grill pan or under a broiler for about 15 minutes, turning occasionally, until blackened all over. Transfer to a plastic bag and let cool. Peel away the skin, discard the seeds, and cut the flesh into quarters, reserving any juices.

Cut the zucchini lengthwise into 1-inch slices, brush with oil, and grill or broil as above for 2 to 3 minutes on each side until lightly charred and softened. Let cool.

Arrange the cooked vegetables in layers inside the loaf, with the goat cheese and remaining pesto in the middle, and the basil on top. Sprinkle the filling with any remaining oil and the pepper juices, and replace the lid.

Wrap the whole loaf in plastic wrap and put it on a plate. Put a board on top, then a heavy food can on top of that to weigh it down. Chill in the refrigerator overnight.

The next day, cut into wedges and serve.

A classic brunch dish given a modern twist with Japanese wasabi paste (horseradish) and sour cream in place of cream cheese.

# bagels with smoked salmon and wasabi sour cream

4 plain bagels

¾ cup sour cream or crème fraîche

2–3 teaspoons wasabi paste

8 oz. smoked salmon

freshly ground black pepper

**To serve (optional)**

chopped fresh chives

lemon wedges

**Serves 4**

Cut the bagels in half and toast lightly on both sides. Put the sour cream or crème fraîche, and wasabi paste, in a bowl and beat until evenly mixed. Add black pepper to taste.

Spread 4 bagel halves with the wasabi mixture. Top with the smoked salmon and chives, if using, then add the remaining bagel halves. Serve with lemon wedges for squeezing, if using.

# taramasalata

Real, homemade taramasalata is a revelation. It is eons away from the lurid, tasteless, manufactured variety sold, alas, worldwide. The real thing requires salted cod's roe—use either the uncolored pressed paste, sold by authentic Greek delis or grocers, or smoked and salted roe, sold by the piece, peeled and chopped (not at all authentic but excellent). Choose a fruity Greek olive oil, if you can, for a profoundly delicious result.

2 tablespoons uncolored pressed salted cod's roe or 4 oz. smoked cod's roe or carp roe

2 slices stale bread, wetted, squeezed dry, then crumbled

freshly squeezed juice of ½ lemon

1 large garlic clove, crushed (optional)

1 cup extra virgin olive oil, preferably Greek

¼ cup chopped red onion, blanched

**Serves 6–8: makes 1⅔ cups**

Put the cod's roe, bread, lemon juice, and garlic, if using, in a food processor. Purée in brief bursts. With the machine running, drizzle in the oil very slowly through the feed tube, to form a pale, dense emulsion. With the machine still running, very gradually drizzle in 3 to 4 tablespoons of boiling water to lighten the mix. Transfer to a bowl and stir in the onions. Serve with black olives, raw fennel, or crisp celery pieces, radishes, or lettuce hearts, and some torn pita breads.

# tapenade

This delicious, intense black paste began life in the South of France as a dip or spread for bread. Capers, anchovies, and tuna are essentials, and Cognac adds particular pungency.

2½ cups salt-cured black olives, pitted (2 cups after pitting)

¼ cup canned anchovies

½ cup canned tuna in olive oil, drained

3 garlic cloves, crushed

½ teaspoon dried oregano or marjoram

⅓ cup pickled or salted capers, drained

¼ cup extra virgin olive oil

2 tablespoons Cognac

sea salt and freshly ground black pepper

**Serves 4–6: makes 2 cups**

Put the pitted olives, anchovies, tuna, garlic, oregano or marjoram, capers, salt, and pepper in a food processor. Blend to a messy paste, then drizzle the oil through the feed tube, in pulsing bursts. Taste, and adjust the seasoning. Drizzle in half of the Cognac and purée again.

Spoon into an airtight container and drizzle the remaining Cognac over the top.

Serve with crusty bread, croûtes, garlicky bread, crostini, breadsticks, or crisp raw vegetables.

# hummus

Lemony, fresh hummus is a delicious Middle Eastern snack food. For 10-minute hummus, use canned chickpeas. Excellent olive oil utterly defines the flavor, so choose a good one.

1 cup dried chickpeas or 2 cups canned

freshly squeezed juice of 1 lemon

2 garlic cloves, crushed

¼ teaspoon salt

2 tablespoons tahini paste (optional)

½ cup extra virgin olive oil, plus extra for serving

freshly ground black pepper

hot paprika, to serve

**Serves 6–8: makes about 2 cups**

If using dried chickpeas, put them in a bowl, cover with boiling water, and leave for 3 hours (or cover with cold water and leave for 8 hours). Drain. Put in a large saucepan, cover with boiling water, bring to a boil, partially cover, and simmer for 1½ to 2½ hours or until the chickpeas are easily crushable and tender. Drain.

Put the chickpeas in a food processor along with the lemon juice, garlic, salt, pepper, and the tahini paste, if using. Blend briefly to a mousse texture. With the machine running, drizzle the oil through the feed tube to form a creamy purée. Taste, and season with more salt and pepper, if necessary.

Serve cool, sprinkled with a little hot red paprika and a trickle of extra virgin olive oil. Serve with crisp lettuce leaves, torn flatbreads, and other crisp raw vegetables.

# three salsas

Salsas give an extra dimension to chicken, meat, and fish, and are incredibly versatile.
The hot pineapple and papaya salsa is good with shrimp or pork, the creamy corn salsa
marries well with chicken, while the tomato and ginger salsa is very good with white fish
or served as a dip with tortilla chips.

# creamy corn salsa

1 ear of fresh corn, husk removed

2 red chiles, such as serrano

1 tomato, chopped

1 garlic clove, crushed

freshly squeezed juice of ½ lime

1 tablespoon maple syrup

2 tablespoons sour cream

sea salt and freshly ground black pepper

**Serves 6**

Preheat an outdoor grill or a broiler until hot. Add the corn and cook for about 15 minutes, turning frequently, until charred on all sides. Let cool.

Add the chiles to the grill or broiler and cook until the skins are charred all over. Transfer to a bowl, cover with a clean cloth, and let cool.

Using a sharp knife, cut down all sides of the corn cob to remove the kernels. Put them in a bowl. Peel and seed the chiles, chop the flesh, and add to the corn.

Stir in all the remaining ingredients, and salt and pepper to taste. Transfer to an airtight container.

# hot pineapple and papaya salsa

½ ripe pineapple

½ large papaya

freshly squeezed juice of 1 lime

1–2 green chiles, such as serrano, seeded and chopped

2 scallions, finely chopped

1 tablespoon chopped fresh mint leaves

1 tablespoon Thai fish sauce (*nam pla*)

**Serves 6**

Peel the pineapple, remove and discard the core, then chop the flesh and put in a bowl, along with any juice.

Peel the papaya, scoop out the seeds, and chop the flesh. Add to the pineapple.

Stir in the lime juice, chiles, scallions, mint, and fish sauce, and set aside to infuse for 30 minutes. Transfer to an airtight container.

# tomato, sesame, and ginger salsa

2 ripe tomatoes, peeled, seeded, and chopped

½ red onion, finely chopped

2-inch piece fresh ginger, peeled and grated

1 garlic clove, chopped

1 tablespoon chopped fresh cilantro

2 tablespoons peanut oil

1 tablespoon soy sauce

1 teaspoon sesame oil

**Serves 6**

Put all the ingredients in a bowl and stir to mix. Set aside to infuse for about 30 minutes. Transfer to an airtight container.

# chicken caesar wrap

This salad has traveled all over the world and many additions to the basic lettuce and croûtons with cheese and anchovy dressing can be found. Transforming the salad into a delicious wrap makes a great idea for a picnic dish.

3 large strips of bacon

8 oz. cooked chicken breast

6 small flour tortillas

1 large romaine lettuce, inner leaves only

12 anchovy fillets in oil, drained and chopped

**Caesar dressing**

1 egg yolk

1 tablespoon freshly squeezed lemon juice

1 teaspoon Worcestershire sauce

½ cup olive oil

¼ cup freshly grated Parmesan cheese

sea salt and freshly ground black pepper

**Serves 6**

Broil or sauté the bacon for 2 to 3 minutes until crisp. Let cool, then cut into thin strips. Shred the chicken into large strips.

To make the dressing, put the egg yolk in a small bowl, add the lemon juice, Worcestershire sauce, and a little salt and pepper, and beat until frothy. Gradually beat in the oil, a little at a time, until thickened and glossy. Add 2 tablespoons water to thin the sauce, then stir in the grated Parmesan.

Lay a tortilla flat on the counter and arrange a few lettuce leaves down the middle. Top with chicken, bacon, anchovies, a spoonful of the dressing, then more lettuce. Wrap the tortilla into a roll, then wrap the roll in a napkin. Repeat to make 6 wraps. Chill the wraps in the refrigerator, then transfer to a cooler until ready to serve.

# meat and poultry

This really is a great dish—tarragon and chicken go together so well. Kids will love it, yet it tastes good enough for adults to tuck into as well. Pesto can be made out of most herbs, so don't hesitate to try your favorites in this recipe and blend to create your own version. If you don't want meat, replace the chicken with steamed vegetables such as zucchini or string beans.

# chicken and tarragon pesto pasta

10 oz. dried penne pasta

¼ cup olive oil

3 cooked chicken breasts, sliced

4 oz. fresh arugula, about 4 cups

sea salt and freshly ground black pepper

**Tarragon pesto**

½ cup pine nuts

1 cup freshly grated Parmesan cheese

a large bunch of tarragon, leaves stripped from the stems and chopped

grated zest and juice of 1 unwaxed lemon

1 garlic clove, finely chopped

¼ cup olive oil

**Serves 4**

Bring a large saucepan of lightly salted water to a boil, add the pasta, and cook for 8 to 9 minutes, or according to the timings on the package, until *al dente* (just cooked but still slightly crunchy in the middle). Drain and refresh the pasta in cold water, then drain thoroughly and toss in the olive oil.

To make the pesto, put the pine nuts in a dry skillet and toast over medium heat until golden and aromatic. Remove from the pan and let cool slightly. Put the toasted pine nuts, Parmesan, tarragon, lemon zest and juice, garlic, and oil in a bowl, and work it until smooth with a stick blender.

Put the pasta, pesto, and chicken, in a large airtight container. Season with salt and pepper and toss well, coating the pasta and chicken evenly with the pesto. Just before serving, add the arugula to the pasta and toss well (don't add the arugula any earlier because the oil will make it wilt).

This recipe is based on the classic Asian dish salt 'n' pepper squid. It is deliciously fragrant and is sure to appeal to the whole family. Serve with a squeeze of lime and sweet chile sauce.

# pepper 'n' spice chicken

1 small chicken

2 tablespoons toasted sesame oil

1–2 limes, cut into wedges

Sweet Chile Sauce (page 45), to serve

**Fragrant Asian rub**

4 whole star anise

2 teaspoons Szechuan peppercorns

1 teaspoon fennel seeds

2 small pieces of cassia bark or 1 cinnamon stick, broken

6 cloves

2 garlic cloves, finely chopped

grated zest of 2 unwaxed limes

1 teaspoon sea salt

**Serves 4**

To make the rub, put the whole spices in a dry skillet and toast over medium heat for 1 to 2 minutes or until golden and aromatic. Remove from the heat and let cool. Transfer to a spice grinder (or clean coffee mill) and crush to a coarse powder. Alternatively, use a mortar and pestle. Transfer the spices to a bowl, add the garlic, lime zest, and salt, and mix well. Set aside to infuse for about 30 minutes.

Cut the chicken into 12 pieces and put in a large dish. Add the rub and sesame oil and work well into the chicken pieces. Cover and let marinate in the refrigerator for 2 hours, but return to room temperature for 1 hour before cooking.

Preheat an outdoor grill and cook the chicken over medium hot coals, or cook under a preheated medium hot broiler, for about 20 minutes, turning after 10 minutes, until the chicken is cooked through. Check by piercing the thickest part of the meat with a skewer—the juices should run clear. Squeeze some lime juice over the chicken and let cool. Serve with the sweet chile sauce.

# chicken sticks with sweet chile sauce

6 boneless, skinless chicken breasts, cut into 10 cubes each

olive oil, for brushing

**Sweet chile sauce**

6 medium-heat red chiles, about 2 inches long, seeded and chopped

4 garlic cloves, chopped

1 teaspoon grated fresh ginger

1 teaspoon sea salt

½ cup rice wine vinegar

½ cup sugar

12 bamboo satay sticks, soaked in water for about 30 minutes

**Serves 12**

**Chicken sticks are always very popular, so it's worth making extra. You can use boneless chicken thighs, but always remove any excess fat and cook them for a little longer.**

To make the sweet chile sauce, put the chiles, garlic, ginger, and salt in a food processor and blend to a coarse paste. Transfer to a saucepan, add the vinegar and sugar, bring to a boil, and simmer gently, partially covered, for 5 minutes until the mixture becomes a thin syrup. Remove from the heat and let cool.

Put the chicken cubes and sweet chile sauce in a bowl and mix well. Cover and chill overnight.

When ready to cook, thread the chicken cubes onto the soaked satay sticks. Heat the broiler to medium-high and brush the rack of the broiler pan with oil. Add the chicken sticks to the rack and cook, in batches if necessary, turning frequently, for 15 minutes, or until the chicken is cooked through. Repeat until all the chicken sticks are cooked. Let cool.

# mini pork and apple pies

Put the pork tenderloin, pork belly, bacon, and chicken livers in a food processor and blend briefly to grind the meat. Transfer to a bowl and mix in the onion, sage, garlic, nutmeg, and a little salt and pepper. Set aside.

To make the pie crust, sift the flour and 1½ teaspoons salt into a bowl. Put the shortening and ½ cup water in a saucepan and heat gently until the shortening melts and the water comes to a boil. Pour the liquid into the flour and, using a wooden spoon, gently draw the flour into the liquid to form a soft dough. Let cool for a few minutes and, as soon as the dough is cool enough to handle, knead lightly in the bowl until smooth.

Divide the dough into 8 equal pieces and roll out 6 of them on a lightly floured counter to form circles 5 inches across. Carefully invert them, one at a time, over an upturned jam jar. Wrap a 12 x 3-inch piece of parchment paper around the outside, then tie around the middle with kitchen string.

Turn the whole thing over so the dough is sitting flat. Carefully work the jar up and out of the pie crust (you may need to slip a small spatula down between the dough and the jar, to loosen it).

Divide the pork filling into 6 portions and put 1 portion into each pie. Peel, core, and dice the apple and put it on top of the filling. Roll out the remaining 2 pieces of dough and cut 3 circles from each piece with a cookie cutter, the same size as the top of the pies.

Put a circle of dough on top of each pie, press the edges together to seal, then turn the edges inward and over to form a rim.

To make the glaze, put the egg yolk and milk in a bowl, beat well, then brush over the tops of the pies. Pierce each one with a fork to let the steam escape, then transfer to a large baking tray. Cook in a preheated oven at 375°F for 45 to 50 minutes until golden. Remove from the oven, transfer to a wire rack, let cool, and serve cold with a green salad.

8 oz. pork tenderloin, chopped

4 oz. pork belly, chopped

3 slices bacon, chopped

1 oz. chicken livers

1 small onion, minced

1 tablespoon chopped fresh sage

1 small garlic clove, crushed

a pinch of ground nutmeg

1 red apple

1 egg yolk

1 tablespoon milk

sea salt and freshly ground black pepper

**Pie crust**

2¼ cups all-purpose flour

¼ cup vegetable shortening

*a jam jar*
*parchment paper and kitchen string*
*a baking tray*

**Serves 6**

The classic Greek kabob, called "souvlaki,"
is a delicious combination of cubed lamb
marinated in red wine with herbs and lemon
juice. The meat is tenderized by the wine,
resulting in a juicy, succulent dish.

# souvlaki with cracked wheat salad

2 lb. boneless lamb,
such as shoulder

1 tablespoon chopped
fresh rosemary

1 tablespoon dried oregano

1 onion, chopped

4 garlic cloves, chopped

1¼ cups red wine

freshly squeezed juice of 1 lemon

⅓ cup olive oil

sea salt and freshly
ground pepper

**Cracked wheat salad**

2½ cups cracked wheat
(bulgur wheat)

¾ cup chopped fresh
flat-leaf parsley

½ cup fresh mint leaves

2 garlic cloves, crushed

½ cup extra virgin olive oil

freshly squeezed juice of 2 lemons

a pinch of sugar

*6 large rosemary stalks or
metal skewers*

**Serves 6**

Trim any large pieces of fat from the lamb, then cut the meat into 1-inch cubes. Put in a shallow, non-metal dish and add the rosemary, oregano, onion, garlic, wine, lemon juice, olive oil, salt, and pepper. Toss well, cover, and let marinate in the refrigerator for 4 hours. Return to room temperature for 1 hour before cooking.

To make the salad, soak the cracked wheat in warm water for 30 minutes until the water is absorbed and the grains have softened. Strain well to extract any excess water, then transfer to a large airtight container. Add all the remaining ingredients, season to taste with salt and pepper, and set aside for 30 minutes to develop the flavors.

Thread the lamb onto large rosemary stalks or metal skewers. Cook on a preheated outdoor grill or under a broiler for 10 minutes, turning and basting from time to time. Let rest for 5 minutes, then wrap in aluminum foil for transporting. Serve with the salad.

Muffins are quick and easy to prepare and these blueberry ones make a lovely sweet treat for a sunny day. If you don't think a muffin tastes the same without a cup of coffee, put a vacuum flask of your favorite brew in the picnic basket.

# blueberry and almond muffins

1½ cups all-purpose flour

1½ teaspoons baking powder

1 teaspoon apple pie spice

½ cup ground almonds or
¾ cup slivered almonds, finely
ground in a food processor

¾ cup sugar

1 egg

1¼ cups buttermilk

½ stick butter, melted

8 oz. blueberries, about 2 cups

2 tablespoons almonds, chopped

*12-cup muffin pan with 10 paper
muffin cups*

**Makes 10**

Sift the flour, baking powder, and apple pie spice into a bowl and stir in the ground almonds and sugar. Put the egg, buttermilk, and melted butter in a second bowl and beat well. Stir the wet ingredients into the dry ones to make a smooth batter.

Fold in the blueberries, then spoon the mixture into the muffin cups in the muffin pan until each one is three-quarters full. Scatter with the chopped almonds and bake in a preheated oven at 400°F for 18 to 20 minutes until risen and golden. Remove from the oven and let cool on a wire rack. Store in an airtight container and eat within 3 days.

# sweet things and drinks

These homemade brownies, deliciously chocolaty and packed with nuts, are real heaven for the taste buds. If you are a true chocoholic, you can top them with a few shavings of white chocolate before serving, if you like.

# fudge brownies

3½ oz. dark chocolate, finely chopped, about ¾ cup

1 stick plus 1 tablespoon unsalted butter, at room temperature

1⅛ cups sugar

1 teaspoon vanilla extract

2 extra large eggs, beaten

⅔ cup all-purpose flour

2 tablespoons unsweetened cocoa powder

a pinch of salt

1 cup pecan halves or walnut pieces

a cake pan, 8 inches square, greased and bottom lined with parchment paper*

**Makes 16**

Put the chocolate in the top of a double boiler, set over steaming but not boiling water and melt gently (do not let the steaming water touch the bottom of the pan). Remove the pan from the heat and let cool while making the brownie mixture.

Put the butter in a large mixing bowl and, using a wooden spoon or electric beater, beat until soft and creamy. Add the sugar and vanilla extract and continue beating until the mixture is soft and fluffy. Gradually beat in the eggs.

Sift the flour, cocoa, and salt onto the mixture, then spoon the melted chocolate on top and gently stir together until thoroughly mixed. Stir in the nuts. Spoon the mixture into the prepared pan and level the surface.

Bake in a preheated oven at 350°F for 30 to 35 minutes until a skewer inserted halfway between the sides of the pan and the center comes out clean—it is important that the center is just set but still slightly soft and not cake-like. Let cool in the pan, then cut into 16 squares.

When cold, remove from the pan and store in an airtight container. They are best eaten within 5 days, or can be frozen for up to 1 month.

*Note  To make removal easier, cut the parchment paper wider than the pan, so it overlaps the edges. After cooling, remove the uncut slab of brownies using the overlapping paper as handles. Work gently, to avoid cracking the top.

# pear gingerbread

3¾ cups all-purpose flour

2 scant tablespoons baking powder

1 tablespoon ground ginger

½ teaspoon baking soda

½ teaspoon salt

¾ cup brown sugar

1½ sticks unsalted butter

½ cup molasses

½ cup golden syrup or corn syrup

1¼ cups milk

1 egg, lightly beaten

2 large pears, peeled, cored, and chopped

*a baking pan, 12 x 8 inches, greased
and bottom lined with parchment paper*

**Serves 12**

Sift the flour, baking powder, ginger, baking soda, and salt into a large bowl. Put the sugar, butter, molasses, golden syrup, and milk in a saucepan and heat gently until the butter has melted and the sugar has dissolved. Pour into the flour mixture, then add the egg, and beat with a wooden spoon until smooth. Fold in the pears, then spoon into the prepared baking pan.

Bake in a preheated oven at 325°F for 1½ hours, or until a skewer inserted into the center comes out clean. Remove from the oven and let the gingerbread cool in the pan for 10 minutes, then transfer to a wire rack to cool completely.

The cooled cake may be wrapped in foil and stored in an airtight container for up to 5 days.

# refrigerator chocolate cake

14 oz. dark chocolate, chopped, about 2½ cups

1 stick plus 1 tablespoon unsalted butter

7 oz. graham crackers, coarsely crushed, about 2 cups

½ cup pine nuts

½ cup shelled pistachio nuts, coarsely chopped

½ cup candied ginger, coarsely chopped

½ cup unsweetened cocoa powder

1 teaspoon ground cinnamon

confectioners' sugar, for dusting (optional)

*a springform cake pan, 9 inches diameter,
greased and bottom lined with parchment paper*

**Serves 12**

Put the chocolate and butter in the top of a double boiler set over simmering but not boiling water, and melt gently (do not let the water touch the bottom of the pan). Stir in all the remaining ingredients except the confectioners' sugar, then spoon into the prepared cake pan. Press the mixture well into the bottom and sides of the pan and smooth the surface with a spatula. Cover with foil and chill overnight in the refrigerator.

When ready to serve, carefully work around the edges of the cake with a spatula and unmold onto a board, removing the paper from the bottom. Dust with confectioners' sugar, if using, and serve in thin sticks.

The cake may be stored in the refrigerator for up to 3 days.

Vanilla syrup transforms this cake into a lovely dessert, but you can also serve it simply with a spoonful of yogurt.

# lemon cake with vanilla syrup and strawberries

1 stick plus 1 tablespoon unsalted butter, softened

⅔ cup sugar

grated zest and juice of 2 unwaxed lemons

2 eggs, lightly beaten

1½ cups all-purpose flour

2 teaspoons baking powder

⅓ cup fine semolina

⅔ cup whole-milk plain yogurt, plus extra to serve (optional)

fresh strawberries, to serve

**Vanilla syrup (optional)**

1 cup sugar

1 vanilla bean

*a springform cake pan, 9 inches diameter, greased and bottom lined with parchment paper*

**Serves 6**

Put the butter, sugar, and lemon zest in a bowl and beat until pale and soft. Gradually beat in the eggs, a little at a time, until evenly mixed. Fold in the flour, baking powder, and semolina, then stir in the yogurt and lemon juice.

Spoon the mixture into the prepared cake pan and bake in a preheated oven at 350°F for about 40 minutes until risen and spongy. The cake is cooked when a skewer inserted into the center of it comes out clean. Let cool in the pan for 5 minutes, then invert onto a wire rack to cool completely.

Meanwhile, to make the syrup, if using, split the vanilla bean lengthwise with a sharp knife. Put the sugar and vanilla bean in a small saucepan and add 1¼ cups water. Heat gently until the sugar has dissolved. Bring to a boil and simmer for about 5 minutes until it becomes syrupy. Remove from the heat and transfer to a vacuum flask for transporting.

To serve, cut the cake into slices, pour the syrup over it, and serve with strawberries. Alternatively, serve with yogurt instead of the syrup.

This cake makes a great treat for picnics and lunchboxes. Feel free to add your favorite nuts or dried fruit instead of the pecans.

# toffee loaf cake

2 cups all-purpose flour

1 teaspoon baking soda

1 cup firmly packed brown sugar

½ cup plain yogurt

½ cup milk

1 extra large egg

1½ tablespoons unsalted butter, plus extra for greasing

½ cup chopped pecans, mixed nuts, or raisins

a loaf pan, 8½ x 4½ x 2½ inches, greased and lined with nonstick parchment paper

**Makes 1 medium cake**

Put the flour, baking soda, and sugar in a bowl. Put the yogurt and milk in a separate bowl. Add the egg and stir well with a fork. Add the melted butter. Pour this mixture into the dry ingredients, mix well with a wooden spoon, then stir in the nuts or raisins.

Spoon the mixture into the prepared pan and bake in a preheated oven at 350°F for 45 to 50 minutes until golden brown. The cake is cooked when a skewer inserted into the center of it comes out clean.

Remove the pan from the oven and let the cake cool in the pan for 10 minutes, then invert the cake onto a wire rack to cool completely. Store in an airtight container and eat within 4 days, or freeze for up to 1 month. Serve in thick slices.

Your dentist won't be happy with this recipe, but you and the kids will be.

# nutty candied apples and candied cherries

2 cups sugar

20 cherries, with stalks

4 apples

⅔ cup chopped nuts

**Serves 4**

Put the sugar in a small saucepan with a scant cup water and bring to a boil. Reduce the heat and simmer until golden. Don't use a spoon to stir the mixture, just swirl the pan: this keeps the heat even and stops the sugar from crystallizing.

When the caramel is golden, remove the pan from the heat. Holding the stems, quickly dip the cherries into the hot caramel, then put them on a sheet of wax paper to set.

Spear the apples onto forks, or use Popsicle sticks. Add the nuts to the caramel and, if it is stiff, heat it through briefly. Dip the apples into the mixture, swirling them around until they are coated all over with the nutty caramel. Put on the wax paper to set for about 5 minutes. Don't let the apples or cherries touch each other or they will stick together.

Wrap the apples and cherries separately in sheets of wax paper to take to the picnic.

# lemon soda with mint and bitters

A delightfully simple drink, ideal for hot summer days.

1 quart lemon soda or lemonade

6 sprigs of mint

Angostura bitters

lemon slices

ice cubes

**Serves 6**

Pour the lemon soda or lemonade into 6 tall glasses, adding a sprig of mint to each one. Add a few drops of bitters, a few slices of lemon, and ice cubes to each glass, then serve at once.

# iced ginger tea

When making iced tea, it's best to add the tea bags to cold rather than boiling water to avoid the unpleasant scum that can appear on the surface. So boil the water, then let it cool before adding the tea.

2-inch piece of fresh ginger, peeled and thinly sliced

4 tea bags

2 limes, sliced

ice cubes

about 2 cups lemon soda or lemonade

**Serves 6**

Put the sliced ginger in a large pitcher, pour 4 cups boiling water over it, and leave until cold. Add the tea bags and chill in the refrigerator for 1 hour.

Strain the tea into a clean plastic pitcher with a lid, or a vacuum flask. Just before serving, add the slices of lime to the tea. Put some ice cubes in 6 glasses, divide the tea between them, and top up with lemon soda or lemonade.

# iced lemon coffee

Iced lemon coffee can be just as refreshing as iced lemon tea on a hot day. It may sound a little strange, but it's very thirst-quenching.

2 cups freshly brewed espresso coffee

sugar, to taste

ice cubes

1 tablespoon freshly squeezed lemon juice

lemon zest, to serve

**Serves 6**

Pour the coffee into a large heat-proof pitcher, add sugar to taste, and stir until dissolved. Let cool, then chill until very cold. Transfer to a vacuum flask to transport.

When ready to serve, half-fill 6 glasses with ice cubes. Add the lemon juice to the coffee, then pour into the glasses and serve with a twist of lemon zest.

# index

# credits

**RECIPES**
**Louise Pickford**  7, 12, 15, 16, 19, 20, 23, 24,
28, 31, 32, 37, 38, 42, 46, 49, 50, 54, 57, 62
**Clare Ferguson**  27, 34, 35
**Fran Warde**  8, 11, 41, 45, 61
**Linda Collister**  53, 58

**PHOTOGRAPHS**
Key: r=right, l=left, c=center

**Ian Wallace**  endpapers, 3, 5, 11, 13–18,
21–22, 25, 29–30, 33, 36, 39, 43, 46–51,
55–58, 62–63
**Debi Treloar**  1–2, 4l cr&r, 8–10, 28, 32, 38, 40,
42, 44–45, 60–61
**Christopher Drake**  4cl, 6, 19, 23
**Martin Brigdale**  26, 52
**Peter Cassidy**  34
**Vanessa Davies**  59

# conversion charts

Weights and measures have been
rounded up or down slightly to make
measuring easier.

**Volume equivalents:**

| American | Metric | Imperial |
|---|---|---|
| 1 teaspoon | 5 ml | |
| 1 tablespoon | 15 ml | |
| ¼ cup | 60 ml | 2 fl.oz. |
| ⅓ cup | 75 ml | 2½ fl.oz. |
| ½ cup | 125 ml | 4 fl.oz. |
| ⅔ cup | 150 ml | 5 fl.oz. (¼ pint) |
| ¾ cup | 175 ml | 6 fl.oz. |
| 1 cup | 250 ml | 8 fl.oz. |

**Weight equivalents:**

| Imperial | Metric |
|---|---|
| 1 oz. | 25 g |
| 2 oz. | 50 g |
| 3 oz. | 75 g |
| 4 oz. | 125 g |
| 5 oz. | 150 g |
| 6 oz. | 175 g |
| 7 oz. | 200 g |
| 8 oz. (½ lb.) | 250 g |
| 9 oz. | 275 g |
| 10 oz. | 300 g |
| 11 oz. | 325 g |
| 12 oz. | 375 g |
| 13 oz. | 400 g |
| 14 oz. | 425 g |
| 15 oz. | 475 g |
| 16 oz. (1 lb.) | 500 g |
| 2 lb. | 1 kg |

**Measurements:**

| Inches | Cm |
|---|---|
| ¼ inch | 5 mm |
| ½ inch | 1 cm |
| ¾ inch | 1.5 cm |
| 1 inch | 2.5 cm |
| 2 inches | 5 cm |
| 3 inches | 7 cm |
| 4 inches | 10 cm |
| 5 inches | 12 cm |
| 6 inches | 15 cm |
| 7 inches | 18 cm |
| 8 inches | 20 cm |
| 9 inches | 23 cm |
| 10 inches | 25 cm |
| 11 inches | 28 cm |
| 12 inches | 30 cm |

**Oven temperatures:**

| | | |
|---|---|---|
| 110°C | (225°F) | Gas ¼ |
| 120°C | (250°F) | Gas ½ |
| 140°C | (275°F) | Gas 1 |
| 150°C | (300°F) | Gas 2 |
| 160°C | (325°F) | Gas 3 |
| 180°C | (350°F) | Gas 4 |
| 190°C | (375°F) | Gas 5 |
| 200°C | (400°F) | Gas 6 |
| 220°C | (425°F) | Gas 7 |
| 230°C | (450°F) | Gas 8 |
| 240°C | (475°F) | Gas 9 |